Beneath My Skin
~ Second Edition ~

Larissa Benfey

*Larissa
Benfey
Press*

Copyright © 2022, 2023 by Larissa Benfey
All rights reserved.

Cover art and internal line art illustrations by Victoria Rusyn

No part of this book may be reproduced in any manner whatsoever without written permission except in the case of brief quotations embodied in critical articles and reviews.

Published by *Larissa Benfey Press*
www.larissabenfey.com

ISBN print: 978-1-7389483-0-7
ISBN electronic: 978-1-7389483-1-4

First edition originally published in 2022 by *BookLeaf Publishing*

Beneath My Skin: Second Edition
First Printing, 2023

to everyone who has made me feel loved—
you're why i'm still here

this is me
my mind, my heart
in words,
imperfect as they seem

imperfect
distorted
a shadow, reflected
a glimpse, a poem, a dream

my eyes, my eyes
they speak as well
not words,
but hopes and pain

i long for you to see within
connect
embrace
remain

it's here again
the fear, again
it thrashes from within

the butterflies
have fangs and claws
that scratch beneath my skin

it doesn't show
i'm silent, calm
on the outside, ever still

years of practice
fronting, hiding
the mask i wear, tranquil

it speaks again
i'm weak again
its whispers still my soul

paralyzed
locked in my mind
will i be swallowed whole?

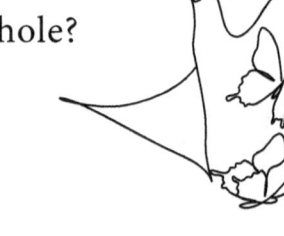

resilience be damned
give me your hand
we'll go through this as one

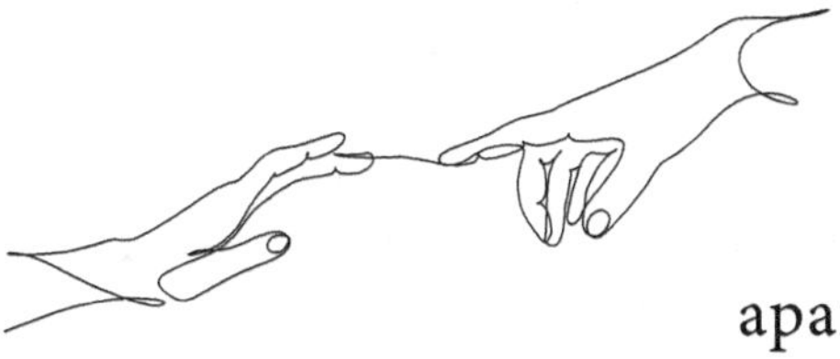

through flood or fire
whatever the mire
apart, we'll come undone

what they don't tell you
is experience leaves bruises
scars, holes, and knots

you may stand up taller
but only once you've felt smaller

and broken

and garbage

and rot

whoever said words
could inflict less pain
than actions
abuse
or touch

was lucky enough
to never hear
the words, you
you are
too much

too pretty
too excited
too boyish
too calm
too skinny
too fat
too lean

too subtle
too intelligent
too blunt
too dumb
too interested
too lazy
too keen

i didn't know the name for it
while it gripped me tight
i knew something was wrong
my cycle was gone
but my body looked so right

'right' to my perverted eyes
whose sense had gone astray
misguided by a cruel
set of standards and rules
that led to wilt; decay

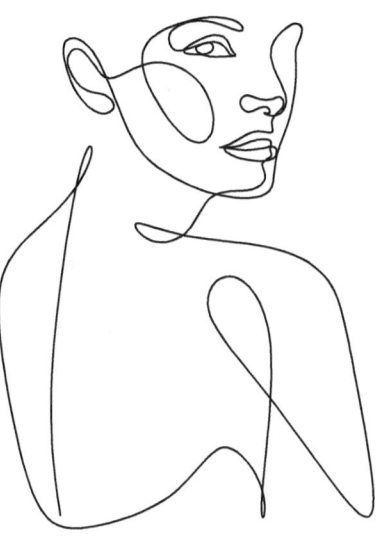

when i learned the monster's name
i'd already won the fight
it scared me still
that i'd managed to kill
this thing with a lethal bite

the years since have taught me
it never stays quite dead
its ghost still haunts me
reviles me and taunts me
it will always hang on by a thread

being understood
is at the bottom of my list
i don't need you to 'get' me
i still expect you to respect me
respect my choice
my space
my life

i stopped seeking
your approval
your acceptance
and your love
when you made it clear
there were conditions
stipulations—

a line
i'd already crossed
by just existing in this body
with this mind
at odds with yours

call me jaded
guarded, hostile
as if i could control
the world i was borne into
as if it didn't mould me
break me
and finally toss me out

being understood
is at the bottom of my list
it fell steadily,
as i did
rooted in the conviction
that these sharp edges
will always be rejected

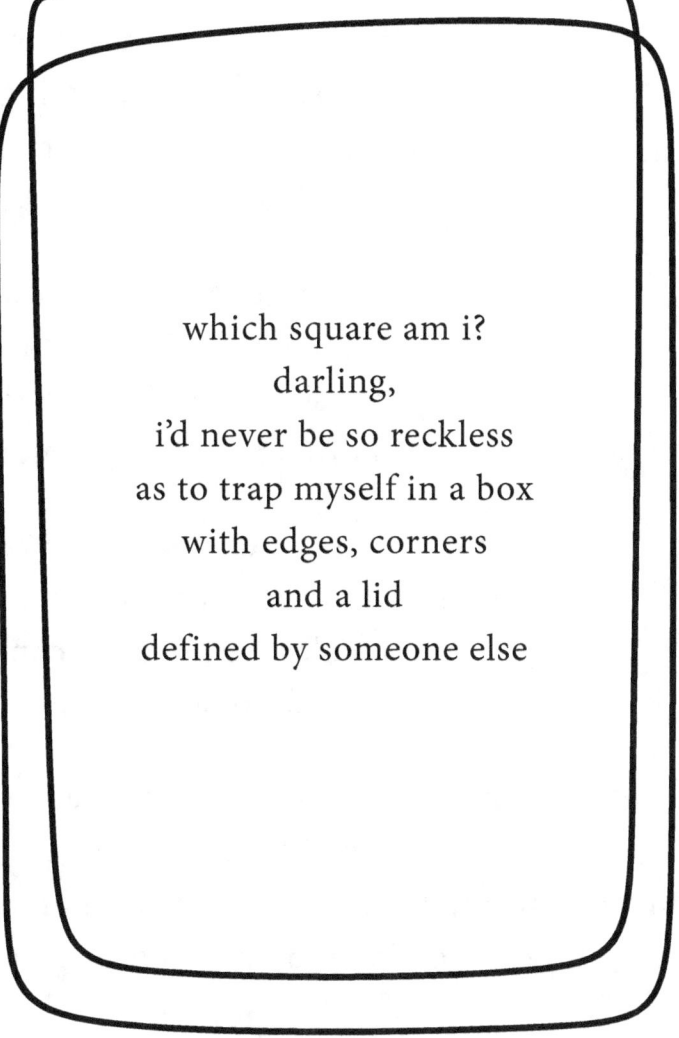

which square am i?
darling,
i'd never be so reckless
as to trap myself in a box
with edges, corners
and a lid
defined by someone else

i have a specific hand towel
it doesn't make me cringe
it doesn't rub my fingerprints
and catch upon my skin

perhaps you've never thought about it
or felt it, as it were
perhaps we see and feel the world
in different hues and blurs

i shut down, shut out, and turn away
when the world is pressed on me
the smallest tasks can become
impossible, suddenly

my limbs get heavy, my mind—a knot
a jumble of thoughts and dread
in a heartbeat, it consumes every part of me
no blood in my veins, just lead

the less our eyes meet

the more of me you see

~ unmasked

i created a mask so convincing
even i couldn't tell
its end from beginning

i wanted to peel each layer away
as if shedding my skin
as if remolding clay

instead, with a spark, i burned it all down
burned my stage and costumes
razed it all to the ground

now there's nothing left but embers and ash
i don't want to rebuild
i'll stay unmasked

~ reset

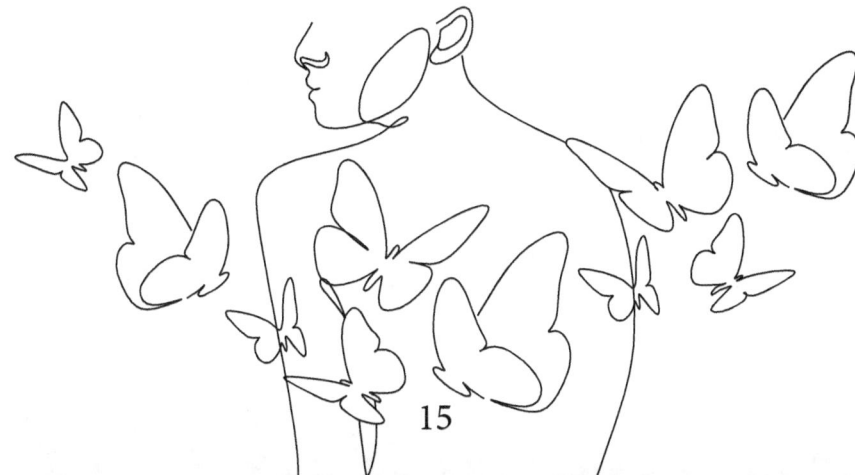

my grandmothers were hurricanes
impossible to ignore

both grandfathers, a gentle breeze
the after and before

did you know you were my garden
before i knew what it meant
to need a refuge, a safe place to stay?

you filled it with laughter
with words soft as petals
it would flower and bloom all day

i used to think you made the birds sing
and the sun shine brighter
in fact—i'm almost convinced you still do

i wish you were here still
to see the garden i'm planting
as i try to become more like you

growing up i heard stories of the
regimented soldier you
once were

strange how they never matched the
silly, doting grandfather i much
preferred

and now all i have are my memories
pure magic, but also
a blur

when i was three,
you sang me lullabies
at seven,
you'd curl my hair
when i was ten,
we'd jazzercize—
you did it with such flair

at fourteen,
you asked what flower
should reside just
outside your door
i told you roses,
and to my delight,
they grew there forevermore

as i got older,
and pursued my dreams
you watched,
oft out of sight
i later discovered
you never faltered
in praying for me ev'ry night

and then, when i was twenty-eight
you drifted
and broke free
my friend and defender,
my grandmother
your strength remains in me

it's hard to put to words a feeling
that envelops you, swallows you whole
especially one so intricately woven
in the fabric of me, body and soul

i'm not lucky enough to have lived a life
free of doubt, sorrow, or fear
but i count myself blessed to have known for a time
a love so severe

severe like a cold winter's day
when the wind can snatch your breath
severe as sore and aching limbs
when they finally find their rest

perhaps words seem insufficient
because he used so few
he expressed his love in quiet ways
and yet, i always knew

it's funny, the parallels you see
in retrospect, looking back
dots connected, lines defined: the big picture
no longer the abstract

you see, my grandad always seemed to be able
to find the silver lining
the positives, the bright side, a flicker in the dark
you might say he spent his life mining

there's a science to it—a method
it requires dedication and patience and skill
and that's just for minerals or rocks or dirt,
with people, it's harder still

yet, here i stand as an example
a sample of his talent
to unearth joy, extract a smile
often from just the faintest glint

his quiet love, ingrained in me
reverberates and echoes here
its impact loud, but what else would you expect
from a love so severe?

you severed the connection
from my body to my mind
tied my worth to just the one
and let the other fall behind

you took away my joy
stole intimacy and grief
convinced me nothing mattered
as much as my belief

~ *what you took from me*

what is it about a rainy day
or city lights at night?

there's something comforting
in the desolate
the dismal and the bleak
in the frigid, vacant glow of lamps
reflected on the street

darkness can envelop you
in a way that light cannot

it feels closer, ever
encroaching, somehow
threatening and benign
or perhaps i just enjoy the thrill
of fear creeping up my spine

'every rose has its thorns'
suggests anything deemed beautiful
is dangerous

i argue

every rose needs its thorns
because beauty does not survive
unless it can defend itself

imagine privilege as a shield
that can vary in size and weight
it will deflect and assuage certain threats
it is capable of changing one's fate

imagine privilege as a key
that's matched to any number of gates
no need to turn back, or find a new route
with the right key, you can keep walking straight

now, your key may not unlock a lot
and your shield may be quite small
but the question lies not in width, height, or amount
it lies in having these items at all

i couldn't escape my monsters
so i befriended them instead
the one hiding in my basement
the one underneath my bed

ignored their horns, their fangs, their claws
and looked them in the eyes
started to see them for who they were
a tangle of fear and lies

i treated them with kindness
i'd smile and laugh and play
turns out that's all they needed
to begin to fade away

they didn't quite disappear
they became a part of me
intertwined with who i was
became the person you now see

my students will say
that i should have wings
that i'll soon fly away
and other such silly things

not angel wings, no
that's not what they think
it has more to do
with all the Red Bull i drink

never allowed my feet to dance
kept them firmly on the ground
the only way i knew to be
from a young age, tightly wound

first one step, then another
my feet began to move
cautiously shuffling, only at first
'til my heart joined in the groove

too soon, too soon, i started to jump
to laugh and love and leap
i leapt high, expecting to fly
but fell flat at his feet

it is not in my character
to give up or give in
i am quite stubborn, you see

in this case, i'm glad
that i tried love again
because now there is 'you and me'

you comple~~te~~ ^(ment) me
and i think i complement you too
i think we make a good fit

you bring grace, perseverance, and strength
i found the right one
you're it

i often wish
naps were like push-ups
and someone told me to d
                              r
                                o
                                    p

and give them twenty

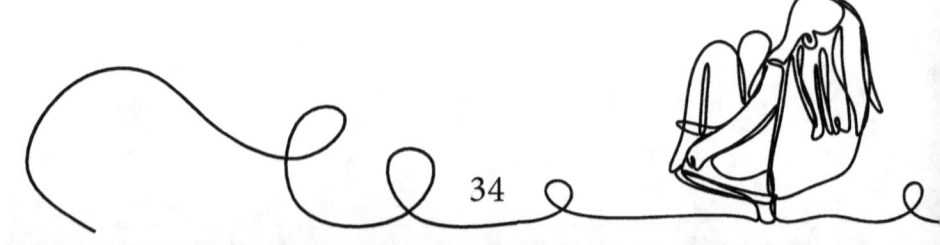

why don't you
make like a tree
and make the planet
a more hospitable place?

it may seem as if you're not mentioned here
in any stanza, symbol, or sheet
but, you see, you are everywhere
infused into every beat

you're in the white space, between every line
you're in the scent, the ink, the rhymes
      you might say it mirrors the love we share
          invisible, yet with me at all times

          i feel it always, wherever i go
      it brings confidence and hope and light
a poem is a canvas too confining, too small
Mom and Dad, you're in everything i write

i feel i've lived a life of almosts
and i don't know what to do
to turn some almosts into nevers
and others into absolutes

almost breakdowns
almost breakthroughs
almost surrenders
almost debuts

almost settling in
almost crying out
almost accepting the rejections
or succumbing to self-doubt

almost throwing in the towel
almost feeling hope again
almost finishing things i started,
things i thought had been in vain

almost wanting new beginnings,
though my heart hangs in the past
almost seeing through the darkness
almost finding light, at last

perhaps it is the almosts
that have gotten me this far
perhaps they're part of all of us
and make us who we are

my father has ingrained in me
many quirks indeed
but perhaps the best among them—
sheer delight seeing people succeed

to see them content, fulfilled, at ease
finding love or just a friend
we're comforted in knowing that
they've found their happy end

i cling to them, these happy ends—
a buoy so i won't drown
while lost in a seemingly endless sea
where injustice and sorrow abound

while it hasn't all been cheery
i hope this book, a lifebuoy too
if these pages brought you solace
then, i'm glad that they found you

www.ingramcontent.com/pod-product-compliance
Lightning Source LLC
Chambersburg PA
CBHW070120110526
44587CB00018BA/3335